Children's Sermons to Go

Children's Sermons to Go

52 Take-Home Lessons About God

Vicky Miller
and
Deborah Raney

Abingdon Press
Nashville

CHILDREN'S SERMONS TO GO: 52 TAKE-HOME LESSONS ABOUT GOD

Copyright © 1998 by Vicky Miller and Deborah Raney

Library of Congress Cataloging-in-Publication Data

Miller, Vicky, 1956–
   Children's sermons to go : 52 take-home lessons about God / Vicky Miller and Deborah Raney.
      p. cm.
   Includes indexes.
   ISBN 0-687-05257-2 (pbk. : alk. paper)
   1. Children's sermons, 2. Christian education—Home training.
   3. Church year sermons. 4. Sermons, American. I. Raney, Deborah.
   II. Title.
   BV4315.M49   1998
   252'.53—dc21   98-35784
                                                                                      CIP

Scriptures quoted from the *International Children's Bible, New Century Version*, copyright © 1986, 1988 by Word Publishing, Dallas, Texas 75039. Used by permission.

01 02 03 04 05 06 07 —10 9 8 7 6 5

MANUFACTURED IN THE UNITED STATES OF AMERICA

Lovingly dedicated to our children:

Samantha Ann and Wesley Rankin

—*VM*

and

Tarl Adam, Tobi Anne,

Trey Andrew, and Tavia Amber

—*DR*

ACKNOWLEDGMENTS

We should like to thank the following people for their assistance with this book:

Our parents, Max and Winifred Teeter, who not only provided the ideas for several of the lessons in this book but also lovingly taught us these principles firsthand as we were growing up.

The Reverend Jeff Miller, of Mitchell Chapel United Methodist Church, Hutchinson, Kansas, whose insight and theological advice were much appreciated.

The Reverend David M. Keazirian of St. Luke Presbyterian Church, Newton, Kansas, who provided the three most clever ideas in the book. (We'll let the reader guess which ones they are!)

Our husbands and children, for their patience while we worked on the manuscript, and for giving us an opportunity to put these lessons to the test.

The children of our churches, who never fail to surprise us with their wit and wisdom.

But Jesus said, "Let the little children come to me.
Don't stop them, because the kingdom of heaven
belongs to people who are like these children." (Matthew 19:14)

CONTENTS

INTRODUCTION

In several years of presenting children's messages in our churches, we have discovered that nothing grabs a child's attention or brings a point home better than a little gift or trinket to carry away from the children's sermon. These treats need not be fancy or expensive. A simple memento can serve as a reminder for the family to talk about and implement the Bible lesson at home throughout the week.

This idea has the added benefit of compelling the usually shy child to join the other little ones at the front of the sanctuary. You will see children's eyes brighten as they listen eagerly to see what this week's surprise might be.

While we believe that the "take-home" angle is a very effective one, many of these sermons may be easily adapted for use without the take-home treat. To that end, the *You will need* section lists only those items necessary for the presentation of the lesson itself. If additional items are needed for the take-home treat, they are listed in the *To take home* section at the bottom of each page.

It is our hope that the ideas in this book will be a starting point for your own creativity. In writing these lessons, we have targeted children ages three to ten, but our own audiences have ranged from two-year-olds to preadolescents. You will know best how to tailor these messages to your particular audience.

May God bless you as you serve him through the infinitely important calling of sharing his truths with the precious children of your church.

Vicky Miller
Deborah Raney

NOTE: In working with children in any setting, safety is a primary concern. Because many of the take-home treats we suggest are edible, we want to remind you to be carefully aware of any special dietary needs represented among the children of your church. It is important to have an alternate item available for those who might be allergic to—or unable to eat—the planned treat.

1. That's the Way the Cookie Crumbles

You will need: • Premeasured ingredients for chocolate chip cookies
   • Small plastic spoons (optional)

Scripture: *1 Corinthians 3:6, 9a   I planted the seed of the teaching in you, and Apollos watered it. But God is the One who made the seed grow. We are workers together for God.*

Today I've brought several things from my kitchen to share with you. Here's a cup of flour. Would anyone like a spoonful? No? Well, how about baking soda? Would you like a bite of that? No? Well, then maybe you'd like to taste some of this shortening. Or a raw egg. Or some salt. *[Be sure not to ask if they want to taste the sugar or chocolate chips! It might be best to keep those two items hidden until it's time to mix them in.]*
Hmm. Nobody seems interested in the things I brought for you to eat today. I wonder—if I mix some of these ingredients together, maybe you might like them a bit better. I brought a bowl and spoon with

me; so let's see what we can come up with. *[Add all the ingredients to the bowl and mix. If you omit the eggs and bring along small plastic spoons, the children may taste the cookie dough at this point.]*

It's interesting that not one of you wanted to taste the flour or the baking soda or the shortening by itself. But when we mixed those things together, we ended up with something that tastes delicious!

This reminds me of God's people. God has given each one of us special talents that we can use to serve him, but we aren't all good at everything. Sometimes the best things happen when God's people come together, with all of us providing the things we do best. Just think how our choir would sound if only one person showed up on Sunday morning. Or if everyone sang exactly the same way. Who would sing the high parts? Who would sing the low parts? Who would play the piano or the organ? All the parts are important, aren't they? And they sound their very best when they are all blended together. Just like our cookie dough!

To take home: Give each child one or two wrapped, baked cookies.

2. Like a Rock

You will need: • A backpack filled with heavy rocks

Scripture: *1 John 1:9   But if we confess our sins, he will forgive our sins. We can trust God. He does what is right. He will make us clean from all the wrongs we have done.*

[Ask for a volunteer, or choose a child who will stand and wear the backpack during the children's sermon. A couple of times throughout the sermon ask the child if the bag is getting too heavy.]
    I have a backpack here that is full of very heavy rocks. *[Unzip the bag and show the children what is inside.]* I would like for you to put this pack of rocks on your back and wear it during our children's sermon this morning. Is it heavy? What do you think it would be like to carry these rocks on your back all day?
    Did you know that sin in our lives is much like carrying these heavy rocks? When you have done something wrong and haven't told anyone about it,

15

how does it make you feel inside? That's right. We feel very unhappy. We might feel sad or worried, or sometimes it might even make us feel sick.

What do we need to do to get rid of those yucky feelings we have inside when we've done something wrong? The Bible says that we need to confess our sins. *Confess* is a word that simply means that we need to tell God about what we have done wrong. Now, when we tell God, it won't be any big news to him, will it? God knows and sees everything we do, so he already knows what we've done even before we tell him. But still, God wants us to tell him. And when we do, we are going to feel a huge load lifted from us. *[Remove the backpack from the child's back.]* Isn't it a relief to get that heavy load off of your back? Just as we took this heavy load off of your back, God can take the load of sin off of us. God has promised to forgive us and to make us clean inside, just as though we had never done that wrong thing. All we have to do is ask! Isn't that good news?

To take home: Paint colorful designs on smooth rocks (or give children pretty polished rocks) to be used as paperweights. "You can take this rock home and use it as a paperweight to remind you that we don't have to carry the weight of our sin. Jesus wants to forgive us—and that's great news!"

3. Do as I Say, Not as I Do

You will need: • A stick of chewing gum
• A tissue

Scripture: *Matthew 23:2-3   "The teachers of the law and the Pharisees have the authority to tell you what the law of Moses says. So you should obey and follow whatever they tell you. But their lives are not good examples for you to follow. They tell you to do things, but they don't do the things themselves."*

[*As you begin the children's sermon, have a piece of gum in your mouth. Chew, crackle, and pop and blow bubbles with it as you talk.*] There's something I want to talk to you kids about this morning. When you are speaking in front of people, you should not be chewing gum. For example, if you have a book report to give at school, it would be very distracting if you were chewing gum and talking at the same time. It doesn't look nice, and it makes it hard to understand what you are saying. Now do you understand what I'm trying to tell you?

[Take the gum out of your mouth and put it in a tissue.]
Have you ever heard the saying "Practice what you
preach"? What does that mean? *[Read scripture.]*

The church leaders in Jesus' day were experts at
telling the people what God's Word *said*, but they
didn't *do* what this Word said. But Jesus said that the
people should still go ahead and obey God's laws.
Sometimes people who teach us about God, such as
our parents, grandparents, pastor, or Sunday school
teachers, don't always do what they are trying to
teach us to do. For example, maybe your dad or your
Sunday school teacher has shown you the verse in
the Bible that says "Be kind to one another," and
then you heard them saying unkind things about
another person. But that does not give you an excuse
to be unkind. Adults who teach us God's word
should do their best to practice what they preach, but
they are human and often make mistakes. You
should remember that the message comes from God,
and it is God that we should obey.

To take home: Give each child a stick of chewing gum.

4. Don't Judge a Book by Its Cover

You will need: • A blank book with a colorful, interesting cover
• A colorful children's book with a plain brown or grey cover
(You might be able to remove an illustrated jacket from a children's book to reveal a plain cover.)

Scripture: *1 Samuel 16:7b* *"God does not see the same way people see. People look at the outside of a person, but the Lord looks at the heart."*

I brought two books with me today. If you saw each of these books in a bookstore or at the library, which one do you think you would choose to bring home to read? So you think you'd like this one with the bright, colorful cover? Well, let's take a look at it and see what it's about. Are you surprised to find that this book is empty? It wouldn't be very interesting reading, would it? What about this one? Let's see what's inside it. Oh, it's full of pictures and it looks like a really exciting story. You know, people are just like these two books. Our outside appearance doesn't always show what is inside. Sometimes people who are beautiful on the outside are not so nice on the inside; and sometimes people who don't look very interesting or nice on the outside might be some of the nicest people you could ever meet. Have you ever heard the expression "You can't judge a book by its cover"? It means that you just can't tell what someone is like on the inside by looking at their outside. God cares about the way we are on the inside—if we're kind and truthful and full of love. God isn't so worried about the kind of clothes we wear or the way we fix our hair. What matters to him is that we are beautiful on the inside—that we treat others with kindness and that the thoughts we have are loving and good. And we should be just like that—not worrying so much about how people look, but getting to know how they really are on the inside.

To take home: Staple several pieces of construction paper together to make small blank books for each child to take home and create their own exciting story.

5. Count the Cost

You will need: • Colorful interlocking building blocks
• Instructions for building a house from these blocks

Scripture: *Luke 14:28-30 "If you wanted to build a tower, you would first sit down and decide how much it would cost. You must see if you have enough money to finish the job. If you don't do that, you might begin the work, but you would not be able to finish. And if you could not finish it, then all who would see it would laugh at you. They would say, 'This man began to build but was not able to finish!'"*

I brought something this morning that is going to be so much fun. How many of you have building blocks something like these at home? Have any of you ever built this little house before? I thought this house looked like it would be fun to make, and the instructions tell you exactly how to do it. *[Begin building the structure following the directions. You should have only enough building blocks to build part of the house.]* Wow! Look how much we've done so far.

Now comes the fun part. We get to start putting in the windows and doors. *[Reach into the empty box.]* Oh no! I don't seem to have any more pieces left. I feel so embarrassed! I got all excited about building this house and look what I ended up with.

Well, maybe we can learn a lesson from this. Let me read you a story from the Bible. *[Read scripture.]* In this story, Jesus really meant that when we say we want to follow him, we must first carefully think about what that means. It is a wonderful thing to follow Jesus, but it's not always easy. The Bible says that if we want to be his follower, we must love him more than anything else. We must love Jesus more than our toys, our favorite TV show, or any of our pets. We must love him even more than we love our father or mother or brothers or sisters. If we get all excited about Jesus and say we want to follow him, but then decide we love other things more than we love him, we'll be like I was with this house. We will be embarrassed and ashamed that we didn't think before we started about what it would take. But deciding to follow Jesus and *sticking* to that decision will bring us the best life we could possibly have.

To take home: You can give each child a small package of interlocking building blocks. These are sold separately, or you may divide a larger set into individual bags.

6. Making Beautiful Music Together

You will need: • A piano with space for the children to gather around

Scripture: *1 Corinthians 12:14, 17-19   And a person's body has more than one part. It has many parts. If the whole body were an eye, the body would not be able to hear. If the whole body were an ear, the body would not be able to smell anything. If each part of the body were the same part, there would be no body. But truly God put the parts in the body as he wanted them. He made a place for each one of them.*

[*Sit at the piano and play slowly up and down the scale to show how every note is different.*] Did you notice that not one of the keys on this piano is exactly like another? They are all special and important. You all know the song "Jesus Loves Me," don't you? I'm going to show you what that song would sound like if all the keys on this piano were exactly the same. [*Play the rhythm of the song using only one note on the piano.*] That sounds pretty dull, doesn't it? It doesn't even really sound like a song, does it? But when we add all the notes—black and white, high and low, major and minor—like this: *[play the song in full harmony]* now the song sounds full and beautiful. God's Word tells us that people are all different, just like the notes on this piano. It says "the body is not made up of one part but of many." Just like the notes on the piano, the world needs all kinds of people working and playing together to make life interesting. When we think we don't like someone because they are different than we are—maybe they have skin of a different color, or maybe their clothes are a little bit unusual, or maybe they are a lot older or younger than we are—we should remember that it takes all kinds of people doing all different kinds of work and play to make our world such a wonderful place to live in.

To take home: Cut musical notes out of paper for the children to take home as a reminder that we each play a special part in our family, our church, and our world.

7. Disappearing Act

You will need: • A melted ice cube in a container

Scripture: *Mark 8:34-35   Then Jesus called the crowd to him, along with his followers. He said, "If anyone wants to follow me, he must say 'no' to the things he wants. He must be willing to die on a cross, and he must follow me. Whoever wants to save his life will give up true life. But whoever gives up his life for me and for the Good News will have true life forever."*

I have a riddle for you. What do a butterfly, cotton candy, and an ice cube have in common? *[Give children a chance to guess.]* Give up? They are all things that you will lose if you try to save them. If you put a butterfly in a jar to keep for yourself, it will soon die. If you lay a stick of cotton candy on the table to save for later, what will happen when you come back to eat it? Right. Cotton candy is mostly air, so you'll come back to a little clump of sugar on a stick. And look here. I put an ice cube in this container this morning to save for the children's time, but look at it now. It's just water. I lost the cube by trying to save it, didn't I?

Our scripture verse talks about losing something when we try to save it. Listen to what Jesus says: *[Read scripture.]* What do you think Jesus means in this verse?

Let me try to help you understand. Did you know that when you were born into this world, you were born wanting your own way? Have you noticed how babies cry when they want something or when they're not happy with something? How many of you like to have your own way? Sometimes even grown-ups are like that. One way we can lose our lives for Jesus is by not always having to have our own way—by letting others have their way at times.

Another way we lose our lives for Jesus is by being willing to be made fun of because we love Jesus. People made fun of Jesus, and he said that they will make fun of us too. But that is also one way we lose our lives for Jesus—by still sticking with him, even when we're made fun of. Do you know what? By losing your life, you are really saving it.

To take home: Give each child a small cube of ice in a paper cup to take back to their seats with them.

8. A Time for Everything

You will need: A paper bag filled with the following:
- A tray and a place setting (plate, napkin, spoon)
- A variety of "junk foods": candy corn, marshmallows, cupcake, etc., including a can of soda pop and a candy bar

Scripture: *Ecclesiastes 7:18   Try to avoid going too far in doing anything. Those who honor God will avoid doing too much of anything.*

It's not quite lunchtime, but I am really getting hungry. I brought a sack lunch with me this morning, so if you don't mind, I'll set my tray up right now.

I'll put my dishes on this tray, and then let's see what I packed to eat. Oh, some marshmallows! Yummy! And here is a cupcake and some licorice. *[Continue pulling junk food out of the bag and arranging it on the plate.]* Oh, here's some candy corn. That's kind of like a vegetable, isn't it? And chocolate chips—my favorite. Now, I'll need something to

drink. Oh good, here's a can of root beer. And for
dessert—a candy bar!

Doesn't this look like a delicious lunch? Do you
think your parents would let you eat a lunch like
this? No? Why not? The truth is, a lunch like this
might taste good for the first five or six bites, but
after that you would probably start feeling rather
sick. And if you really did eat the whole thing, you'd
have a tummy ache you wouldn't forget for a long
time.

You see, it's okay to eat sweets once in a while, but
if the only things we ever ate were sweets, pretty
soon our bodies would be missing out on the important foods they need to make us strong and healthy.

The Bible says there is a time for everything. We all
need sleep, but if all we ever did was sleep, we
would get pretty bored, wouldn't we? And it's good
to go to school and church and learn important
things, but we also need time to play and relax, don't
we?

God made our lives full of interesting things, but
we need to find just the right balance and just the
right time for everything. That's the way God
planned it, and we can be certain that this is the best
way because God is the one who made us!

To take home: Put the candy bar and soda pop back in the bag,
and then let each child choose one item from your plate.

☼9. Read the Label

You will need:
- A can of spinach or some other "yucky" vegetable
- A label from a can of peaches or another "yummy" fruit

Scripture: *Matthew 12:34b   The mouth speaks the things that are in the heart.*

I brought a can of spinach with me today. Now, your parents probably will not like to hear me say this because spinach is very, very good for you, but I must confess: I can't stand spinach! I think it is absolutely yucky! Well, I had a great idea when I saw this can of spinach sitting right beside a can of peaches in my cupboard. I decided that since I hate spinach so much, I could just peel the label off of a can of peaches and put the peach label on this spinach can, because I *love* peaches. Don't you think that was a good idea? Now I can open up this can and eat the delicious peaches inside. What? You don't think there are peaches in here now? *[You may want to have a can opener handy in case there are any skeptics in the crowd!]* Well, I'm afraid you're right. Putting a different label on this can doesn't change the fact that it's full of spinach, does it?

You and I are a little bit like this can. It's what is inside our hearts that really matters. We can put on a nice "label," dress and act nice and sweet on the outside, but if our inside thoughts are ugly and unkind, we can't hide that from Jesus. So let's be sure that what's inside our hearts is something sweet and good—like good thoughts, love, and kindness.

To take home: Send each child home with a single serving can of peaches. You may have to reassure them that you haven't switched the labels! If one child claims to like spinach, you can send that home with him too!

10. Now You See It

You will need:
- A folded fan
- Perfume in a spray bottle or atomizer
- Recorded music (preferably to be played on cue over the church's sound system)

Scripture: *Romans 1:20a   There are things about God that people cannot see—his eternal power and all the things that make him God.*

Do you know what the word *invisible* means? If something is invisible, that means you cannot see it. The Bible says that there are some things about God that we can't see. I brought some things with me today that I think will help you understand this better. The first thing I brought is a fan. If I wave the fan like this, can you feel the air that the fan makes? Now, that air is invisible, isn't it? You cannot see it, but you can see what the movement of the air does. It makes a cool breeze on your faces, and it blows your hair around. So the air is invisible, but we can still see what it does.

Close your eyes for just a moment. *[Spray a light mist of perfume in the air.]* Now open your eyes and tell me if you smell a sweet scent in the air. Do you smell that? Even though you can't see the perfume that made that nice smell, your nose can certainly tell that there is perfume in the air.

There is one more thing I want to show you about God's invisible qualities. *[Have music played from the church's sound system at this point.]* Can any of you see that beautiful music? No, we can't see music, can we? But there is no doubt that the music is there. We can hear the beautiful sound even though we can't see it.

In some ways, God is like the air that the fan moved, the smell of the perfume, and the sound of the music. Even though we can't see God or touch God with our hands because he is invisible, still, we know that God is there because of the things we see around us. When we see a beautiful sunset, we know that God made it. When we smell a sweet flower, we know that God made it grow. When we hear the choir singing beautiful music, we know that God gave them the music and the voices to sing.

To take home: Give each child a small folded fan to take home with them.

11. Chain Reaction

You will need: [If you do not use the take-home item, you will not need any materials to present this lesson.]

Scripture: *John 1:40-41 These two men followed Jesus after they heard about him from John. One of the men was Andrew. He was Simon Peter's brother. The first thing Andrew did was to find his brother, Simon. He said to Simon, "We have found the Messiah." ("Messiah" means "Christ.")*

When you have some exciting news, what is the first thing you want to do? That's right. We usually want to tell someone else. Our Bible story today is about someone who found out some very good news. This man's name was Andrew. One day Andrew began to follow Jesus. When Jesus saw Andrew following him, he asked him what he wanted. Andrew wanted to know where Jesus was staying, and Jesus took Andrew and another follower to that place. They spent the whole day with Jesus. After they left, the very first thing Andrew did was to find his brother, Simon Peter, so he could tell him all about Jesus.

Andrew and Peter followed Jesus for the next three years that Jesus was on earth. After Jesus died, rose again, and then went to be with God in heaven, they spent their lives telling other people about Jesus. I imagine that many of the people they told about Jesus in turn told others.

I'd like for us to do a little experiment to see how many people could hear about Jesus if just one of us begins to tell the good news. *[Select one child to tell another child that "Jesus loves you" or "Jesus is alive." Have these two children tell two more and so on until all of the children have been told the message. Then instruct the children to go out into the congregation and tell one person the message, and then come back to the front. As the children go out, instruct the congregation to pass on the message they have been given until the entire church has heard the good news.]*

To take home: Have lengths of colorful ribbon or yarn ready to tie around each child's wrist as they return to the front. "This ribbon is to remind you that we need to tell others that Jesus loves them. Then you can invite them to church to learn about and worship Jesus. This is how our church can grow and others can come to know Jesus."

12. 70 x 7

You will need:
- Exactly 490 small colorful candies (Usually about a pound-and-a-half of Skittles or M&Ms will yield this number.)
- A small paper bag to pour the candies from
- A transparent bowl or wide-mouth jar

Scripture: *Matthew 18:21-22   Then Peter came to Jesus and asked, "Lord, when my brother sins against me, how many times must I forgive him? Should I forgive him as many as 7 times?" Jesus answered, "I tell you, you must forgive him more than 7 times. You must forgive him even if he does wrong to you 77 times."*

When someone does something that makes us feel bad, they should tell us they are sorry, shouldn't they? But whether or not they apologize and ask us to forgive them, Jesus wants us to overlook what they did and try to be friends again. That is what forgiveness means. Now, if someone really is hurting you, you need to tell a grown-up you can trust to keep you safe. But suppose a friend has hurt your feelings, not just once, but maybe even two or three times. How many times do you think we should forgive someone? The Bible tells how the disciple named Peter asked Jesus just that question. Peter said, "Should I forgive someone up to seven times?" And do you know what Jesus told him? Jesus said that Peter should forgive not just seven times, but *seventy times seven! [Count out seven candies into the container.]* Now this is how many seven is. But this *[now pour 483 more candies into the container. The more full the container looks, the better the point will come across!]* is what 70 x 7 looks like! That's 490 candies! It's quite a lot, isn't it? I think maybe Jesus was trying to say that we should *always* forgive people when they do wrong things to us. We know that no matter how many times *we* sin, Jesus still loves us and forgives us, so we should do the same thing for others, shouldn't we?

To take home: Give each child a small, clear plastic bag of candies. Tie the bag with ribbon and attach a small tag with the scripture printed on it. (You can say: "490 candies might give you a bad tummy ache, but here are just a few to remind you of this important lesson about forgiveness.")

13. Up, Up, and Away

You will need: • Balloons (at least two each, in various shades of red, pink, yellow, black, brown, and white, and filled with helium.) Tie a long string to each balloon, and make sure you have enough for each child to take one home.

Scripture: *As the children come to the front of the church, have the congregation sing "Jesus Loves the Little Children."*

Do you like this big bunch of balloons I brought today? Aren't they colorful? I want to tell you a story about these balloons. A bunch of balloons were playing together in the park on a beautiful sunny day. They were flying around and having a great time together when, all of a sudden, the pink balloon looked at his friend the brown balloon. "Hey!" he said, "you look different than I do! I don't think I want to play with you anymore." He left the brown balloon all alone in a corner of the park and went off to find some other pink balloons to play with. *[As you tell the story, have a different child hold each color*

*group away from the original bunch so the balloons are
"acting out" the story.]* The black balloon overheard
what the pink balloon said. He'd never noticed it
before, but the pink balloon was right. The brown
balloon *did* look different. He looked over at his
friend the yellow balloon. Come to think of it, the
yellow balloon looked different too—so pale
and ... well, yellow. *He* was a beautiful, shiny black
color. And so he decided that he, too, would only
play with balloons that looked like him. He left the
yellow balloon alone and flew off to find some other
black balloons to play with. The red balloon noticed
that all of his balloon friends had left the bunch and
gone off in corners to play with their own kind. He
looked at the sky where once a bright colorful bunch
of balloons had been and he felt sad. So he went over
to the pink balloon and invited him to play. Then he
invited all the other balloons to play. Soon they were
all playing happily together and the sky was once
again filled with a beautiful rainbow of colors.

Jesus loves every one of us, no matter what we
look like. He wants us to love each other too; and to
be friends with everyone, even if they might be a little different from us.

To take home: Give each child one of the balloons to take home.
(Or hand them out at the door after church.)

14. The Gift That Keeps Giving

You will need: • Clear drinking glass filled half full of water
• Ten or fifteen colorful marbles

Scripture: *Ephesians 3:17b-19   I pray that your life will be strong in love and be built on love. And I pray that you and all God's holy people will have the power to understand the greatness of Christ's love. I pray that you can understand how wide and how long and how high and how deep that love is. Christ's love is greater than any person can ever know. But I pray that you will be able to know that love. Then you can be filled with the fullness of God.*

How many of you like to get presents? It's a lot of fun to open a gift, isn't it? How many of you like to give presents? It feels good to give something to someone—a gift that you know they will like and enjoy, but if it happens to be something that you would like to have for yourself, it's sometimes hard to give it away.

I want to tell you about a very special gift. This gift is special because the more you give it away, the more you have to keep for yourself! Sounds like a pretty neat present, doesn't it? Can anyone guess what that present is? It's love!

I have a glass of water with me today. You can see this glass is filled halfway up with water. We are going to pretend that the water in this glass represents love. I also have some marbles with me. Let's pretend that this shiny blue marble is you. We'll put "you" in the glass so that you are surrounded by love. Now, I'm sure your parents love you very much, so we'll put a marble in with you to represent them. Some of you might have brothers and sisters that you must share your parents' love with, so we'll put some "brother" and "sister" marbles in the glass as well. And we'll put in some grandmas and grandpas and cousins and some other friends. Can you see what's happening to the "love"? That's right! It's growing. The love doesn't get used up when it has to be shared by so many people. No, instead it grows and grows until, if we share it with enough people, soon it would spill right out of the cup. Let's thank God for the wonderful gift of love he gave us. It never runs out!

To take home: From white paper, cut out shapes like the drinking glass you used for the sermon. Give the children several round, colorful stickers to put "in" their glass.

15. Lost and Found

You will need: [If you do not use the take-home item, you will not need any materials to present this lesson.]

Scripture: *Luke 15:4-7*   *"Suppose one of you has 100 sheep, but he loses 1 of them. Then he will leave the other 99 sheep alone and go out and look for the lost sheep. The man will keep on searching for the lost sheep until he finds it. And when he finds it, the man is very happy. He puts it on his shoulders and goes home. He calls to his friends and neighbors and says, 'Be happy with me because I found my lost sheep!' In the same way, I tell you there is much joy in heaven when 1 sinner changes his heart. There is more joy for that 1 sinner than there is for 99 good people who don't need to change."*

How many of you have ever been to an amusement park or carnival? What is your favorite part about a carnival? What do you think would happen if you got lost at an amusement park? Do you think your parents would go home without you? Or do you think they would be pretty worried and do everything they could to find you? Well, what if you had twelve brothers and sisters? Do you think your parents would still try to find you, or would they just say, "Oh, we have plenty of other kids; let's just go on home?" Of course they wouldn't say that, would they? No matter how many children there might be in your family, each one of you is special. I'm sure your parents would do everything they could to find their lost child.

When Jesus was on earth, crowds of people came to hear him talk. Many of those who came were people who did bad things. Jesus was glad that these people came to hear him, and sometimes he even ate a meal with them. Some people who went to church all the time got upset about this. They didn't think Jesus should spend time with those kinds of people. So Jesus told them this story: *[Read scripture.]* Jesus wanted these people to know that when one person who does bad things decides to quit doing bad things and follow him, there is more joy in heaven than for ninety-nine people who don't need to change.

To take home: Give each child a cotton ball to remind them of the lost sheep. If you like, you can glue the cotton ball to a sheep cut from heavy paper, using the pattern on this page. You could also place a self-adhesive magnet on the back of each sheep.

16. Plenty to Go Around

You will need: • Fish-shaped crackers

Scripture: *Luke 9:11-17*   *[The scripture is told in story form.]*

Have you ever been really, really hungry? Isn't it a great feeling when you finally get to eat something and your tummy is full? I want to tell you a Bible story about some people who were hungry. It was late in the afternoon and Jesus had been talking to a large crowd of people. He had also healed those who were sick. Jesus' disciples came to him and told him to send the people away so that they could go into the nearby towns to find food and a place to stay. Jesus told his disciples to give them something to eat. But the disciples told Jesus that they only had five loaves of bread and two fish. Jesus told the disciples to have the people sit down in groups of fifty. Then Jesus looked up to heaven, gave thanks for the food, and divided the loaves and fish. He gave them to his disciples to pass out to the people. *[Give each child a cracker.]* All the people got as much as they wanted to eat. There was even food left over. This was a wonderful miracle, wasn't it? Jesus fed over five thousand people with just five loaves and two fish. But there is an even greater miracle that Jesus does. Just like when we're hungry for food we have an ache in our tummies, without Jesus, we have an ache in our hearts. That feeling is there because of the sin in our lives. The miracle is that Jesus takes away that sin— that hungry feeling—we have in our hearts. Nothing except Jesus can take away that ache. When he comes into our lives, he fills our hearts with peace, joy, and happiness.

To take home: Give each child a package of the fish-shaped crackers to take home.

17. Turn on the Lights!

You will need: • Someone to turn the lights in the church off and on

Scripture: *John 8:12   [Jesus] said, "I am the light of the world. The person who follows me will never live in darkness. He will have the light that gives life."*

I would like everyone to sit very still and stay in your places because in just a few minutes it is going to get very dark in here. Are you ready? *[Once all the children are settled, have someone turn all the lights out. Make sure it isn't scary for younger children, especially if your church has no windows to the outside.]* Wow! It's hard to see in here now that the lights are turned off, isn't it? If we were to try to walk around the sanctuary right now we would probably have a lot of problems. We might trip and fall. We might bump into someone else. I suppose we could even get lost in this big room.

Let's turn the lights back on now so we can see what we are doing. That's better! Jesus said that he is

45

the Light of the world. Just as the lights in this room
keep us from stumbling and falling and getting lost,
so Jesus can keep us safe. He really is like a light
because he helps us to see things clearly and he helps
us not to get lost in sin. I'm so glad that Jesus came
to be a light in our darkness, aren't you?

To take home: Give the children special glow-in-the-dark stickers
to take home as a reminder that Christ is the Light of the world.
These stickers are available at many grocery and stationery
stores.

18. United We Stand

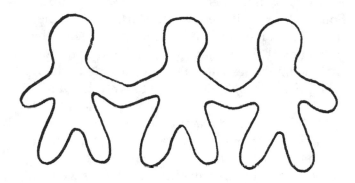

You will need: • Three children to volunteer

Scripture: *1 Corinthians 1:10-13a   I beg you, brothers, in the name of our Lord Jesus Christ. I beg that all of you agree with each other, so that you will not be divided into groups. I beg that you be completely joined together by having the same kind of thinking and the same purpose. My brothers, some people from Chloe's family have told me that there are arguments among you. This is what I mean: One of you says, "I follow Paul"; another says, "I follow Apollos"; another says, "I follow Peter"; and another says, "I follow Christ." Christ cannot be divided into different groups!*

How many of you ever argue or fight with your brothers or sisters or friends? How many of you have ever thought or said, "I'm better than you are"? There are some people in our Bible lesson this morning who sound a lot like this. The apostle Paul wrote to some people in the church in a town called Corinth, and in this letter he scolded them for arguing. Some of them were saying, "I follow Paul."

Others were saying, "I follow Peter." And still others said, "I follow Christ. Beat that!" By saying these things, they were really saying "I'm better than you are."

I need three volunteers to help me out. Your goal is to walk down the aisle to the back of the church. Sound easy? Well, before you start, listen to the directions. First you have to lock arms. Then the person on the right has to begin walking to the right, the one on the left has to begin walking to the left, and the one in the middle has to walk forward. Ready? Go!

It's impossible to reach your goal when you're all going in different directions, isn't it? When the people in Corinth argued, and when we argue in our families, at school, or in church, it's as if we're all going in different directions and none of us can reach our goal. Who can tell me what our goal as Christians should be? We should try to become more like Jesus, shouldn't we? So let's try to do what Paul said: not argue and join together to live for Jesus.

To take home: Finger traps, woven straw tubes that trap your fingers when you place one finger from each hand inside and pull in opposite directions. (These may be purchased inexpensively from a party or carnival supply store or catalog.) You might demonstrate how the finger trap works, asking "Can you see what happens when my fingers pull against each other? They both get trapped and neither one of them can make any progress. It's the same for Christians. If we try to go in different directions, we wind up not getting anywhere at all. So let's all work together and we'll accomplish great things for the Lord!"

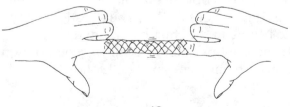

19. Obey the Rules

You will need: • An example of rules that you have at home or an object that relates to one or more of those rules

Scripture: *Psalm 119:1-2 Happy are the people who live pure lives. They follow the Lord's teachings. Happy are the people who keep his rules. They ask him for help with their whole heart.*

How many of you have rules at your house? What are some of the rules that you have to follow in your family? *[Give a personal example of a rule in your family, such as the following:]* Anyone who knows me very well knows that I'm pretty picky about the TV. When we got our TV, the first thing my husband and I did was sit down and make some rules concerning the TV. *[Tell about or read some of the rules.]*

Do you think we made these rules because we want to be the meanest parents in the neighborhood? Do you think when we made these rules we were thinking, "Let's see how much fun we can take away from our kids. Let's see how miserable we can make their lives"? No, even though our kids don't always like the rules, we were actually trying to help them. Do you think it would be good for you if your parents allowed you to watch TV from the time you woke up until the time you went to bed? It wouldn't be healthy for your body, your mind, or your spirit, would it?

God has also given us some rules to live by. Where do we find these rules? That's right, they are in the Bible. Do you think God gave us these rules to be mean or to take all of our fun away? Of course not. Just like your parents, God set these rules because God knows what's best for us. After all, God made us, so who else would better know what would make us the happiest and healthiest people we could possibly be? *[Read scripture.]*

To take home: Give each child a bookmark on which the Ten Commandments are printed. These are widely available at Christian bookstores.

20. Signed, Sealed, Delivered

You will need: • An addressed, stamped thank you note on which you have written a thank-you note to Jesus

Scripture: *1 Chronicles 16:8-9   Give thanks to the Lord and pray to him. Tell the nations what he has done. Sing to him. Sing praises to him. Tell about all the wonderful things he has done.*

Have any of you ever received a special letter in the mail? There are a lot of different kinds of letters that we can get in the mail. Sometimes we get what is called "junk mail." These letters are advertisements, and they usually aren't very important or special. But then there are letters that we get from our friends or our family. Those kinds of letters have special importance because they are from people we love and they tell us what is happening in those people's lives. Have you ever received an invitation in the mail? Now, an invitation is extra special because it asks us to come to a special party or event.

All of these kinds of letters are nice to receive, but the letter I brought with me today is still another special kind of letter. Let's open it up and see what kind of letter it is. This is a thank-you note. Have you ever gotten a birthday gift or a Christmas present that you needed to write a thank-you note for? I'm sure that when the person who gave you the gift received your thank-you letter, it made them very happy to know that you liked your present and that you showed your appreciation by writing to them.

As I thought about thank-you letters this week, I thought that if ever anyone deserves a thank-you note, it is Jesus. He has done so much for each one of us that we should not forget to thank him. So I wrote a thank-you note to Jesus. Now, Jesus doesn't have a mailbox in heaven where he gets his letters, but he *has* given us a special way to talk to him. That special way is prayer. Why don't we read this thank-you note together as a prayer to the Lord.

To take home: Give each child a blank thank-you note to take home to write their own letter to Jesus thanking him for their blessings.

21. All's Not Fair

You will need: • An item related to an unfair experience you have had

Scripture: *1 Peter 2:19, 21-23   A person might have to suffer even when he has done nothing wrong. But if he thinks of God and bears the pain, this pleases God. That is what you were called to do. Christ suffered for you. He gave you an example to follow. So you should do as he did. "He did no sin. He never lied." People insulted Christ, but he did not insult them in return. Christ suffered, but he did not threaten. He let God take care of him. God is the One who judges rightly.*

Can you think of a time when you were punished or got in trouble for something you didn't do? It's upsetting to be treated unfairly, isn't it?
[Share a personal story of a time when you were unjustly accused, using a related object as a visual aid.]
Example: I remember a time when I was about four years old. My parents went out for the evening and left my sisters and brother and me with a babysitter. She gave us each two cookies, but that was all we

were allowed to have. I ate one of my cookies and saved the other one to eat later. But later, when the babysitter saw the cookie I had saved, she thought I had snuck into the cookie jar and taken another one. She got mad at me and blamed me for something I didn't even do! That happened a long time ago, but I can still remember how upset I was at being accused of something I didn't do. We don't easily forget the times we were treated unfairly, do we?

Was Jesus treated fairly? Our Bible lesson tells us that Jesus never sinned. He never told a lie or did anything wrong, and yet many people said wrong and hurtful things to him. But he never said hurtful things back. Jesus never said "I'll get even with you!" or "You're going to pay for that!" No. He suffered for each one of us, and we should follow his example. Jesus knew that God is the one who does the right and fair thing. You see, if we complain about being treated unfairly, if we always try to get even, we will be acting no differently than people who don't follow Jesus. But if we suffer the hurt or pain and leave the getting even to God, people will notice that we are different, and this will give us a chance to show them Jesus.

To take home: An item that relates to your unfair experience. For example, with the story above, you could give each child two cookies.

22. Knock-Knock

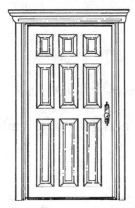

You will need: • Motel door hanger that says "DO NOT DISTURB"

Scripture: *Revelation 3:20* *"Here I am! I stand at the door and knock. If anyone hears my voice and opens the door, I will come in. . . ."*

Have any of you ever stayed overnight in a hotel or motel? It's fun sometimes to go on vacation and get a chance to stay all night in a place where housekeepers or maids make the bed and clean the room for you. I'll bet your parents really appreciate a chance to not have any beds to make or laundry or housecleaning to do.

Sometimes hotel rooms will have signs like this to hang on the door. Have you ever seen one of these? It's called a door hanger and the words say "DO NOT DISTURB." That means when this sign is hanging on your door you don't want anyone to bother you or to knock on your door—perhaps because you are sleeping, or maybe because you just need some peace and quiet.

The Bible talks about someone knocking on a door, except the door this verse is talking about is the door to your heart. The Bible tells us in Revelation that Jesus is knocking on the door to each of our hearts. When he knocks on the door to *your* heart, I hope you won't have a "DO NOT DISTURB" sign hanging up. Instead, we should open the doors to our hearts wide and welcome Jesus in. In fact, maybe we could have a different kind of sign hanging on our hearts. *[Show the children the take-home item, a door hanger that says "WELCOME, JESUS! COME IN!"]* How about a sign like this? I think that would make Jesus very happy.

To take home: Cut door hangers from cardboard. On each one, print "WELCOME, JESUS! COME IN!" Say: "You can hang this sign on your bedroom door at home to remind you that Jesus wants you to open the door to your heart and come into your life."

23. Rest Stop

You will need: • A pillow

Scripture: *Mark 6:30-31   The apostles that Jesus had sent out to preach returned. They gathered around him and told him about all the things they had done and taught. Crowds of people were coming and going. Jesus and his followers did not even have time to eat. He said to them, "Come with me. We will go to a quiet place to be alone. There we will get some rest."*

How many of you have seen the television commercial about the Energizer bunny? What do they say about this bunny? Right. "He keeps going and going and going." God didn't make us like the Energizer bunny. We can't keep going and going and going without certain things. What do we need to keep going? Food, water, exercise, and rest. Rest is what I want to talk about today. That's why I brought my pillow with me. Do any of you ever have to take a nap? Some of you have outgrown naps, but you'll enjoy them when you get to be my age!

Sometimes we play so hard and are having so much fun that we don't want to stop and rest. But what happens when you don't rest? You get tired and grouchy and hard to live with, don't you? Your parents or grandparents know that you need rest, and when they ask you to take a nap or cut back on some activities, they are doing what's best for you.

Did you know that when Jesus was on earth he needed rest too? Jesus' disciples had just come back from preaching and healing. They were telling Jesus about all they had done and taught. So many people were coming and going that Jesus and his followers did not even have time to eat. Listen to what Jesus tells his disciples: "Come with me. We will go to a quiet place to be alone. There we will get some rest." If Jesus needed to rest, don't you think that we need to take time to rest also?

To take home: Give each child several marshmallows in a plastic bag to take home. "Marshmallows have always reminded me of little pillows, so I'm giving each of you some to remind you of our lesson today."

24. Yes, No, Maybe

You will need: • Candy or another treat for each child
• Several "junk" items (an old sock, bottle cap, paper clip, etc.)
• A paper bag

Scripture: *Psalm 34:15 The Lord sees the good people. He listens to their prayers.*

I have a game I'd like you to play with me this morning. I brought a bag with different things inside. Your part in the game is to ask me, "May I please have something from your bag?" Ready? [*As each child asks the question, give a treat to some, give a "junk" item to others, tell some children "no, you may not have anything right now," and tell others "wait a while and then I will give you something." Make sure the very young children get a treat, as they might not understand the game.*]

How did you like this game? [*Ask the children who got "junk" items how they felt about what they got. Then*

ask the ones who were told "no" or "wait" how they felt.]
I wonder if this is how we sometimes feel when we pray to God. Do you ever wonder, "Why did that person get what they prayed for and I didn't?" Sometimes we get the idea that the only time God answers our prayers is when the answer is "yes" or when the answer is exactly what we had in mind.

Did you know that God sometimes answers us by saying "no"? Or he might ask us to wait a while. God also might answer in a way that is totally different from what we were expecting. Let's go back to the game we played. Maybe I know that (child's name) is allergic to this candy, so I told her "no." And maybe I knew that (child's name) had eaten five doughnuts for breakfast and that eating this candy would make him sicker than he already is. So I told him to wait. And maybe (child's name)'s dad will lock the keys in his car after church and this paper clip will be just what he needs to open the lock. What I'm trying to say is that God knows what is best for us and we can be sure that God hears our prayers. We need to learn to trust God and believe that our prayers will always be answered in the way that is best for us.

To take home: Give each child a "good" treat from the bag.

25. The Cornerstone

You will need: • A set of children's building blocks

Scripture: *Luke 6:47-48   "Everyone who comes to me and listens to my words and obeys is like a man building a house. He digs deep and lays his foundation on rock. The floods come, and the water tries to wash the house away. But the flood cannot move the house, because the house was built well."*

[*As you read or talk about the scripture verse, begin to make a tower by stacking the building blocks one atop another.*] The verse today talks about Christians being like houses that are built on strong foundations. The beginning building block of a house—or the foundation—is sometimes called the cornerstone. The cornerstone is the most important part of any building. If the cornerstone is not straight and strong, it might shift or crumble when a flood or a strong wind comes along.

This bottom block is the foundation or the cornerstone of the tower I'm building. What happens when you pull the cornerstone out from under the tower? *[Let one of the children pull the bottom block out.]* When we lose the foundation, the whole building comes tumbling down, doesn't it?

I'm going to read another scripture that talks about this very important foundation. Listen carefully and see if you can tell me who should be the cornerstone of *our* lives. *[Read Ephesians 2:19b-20 "Now you are citizens together with God's holy people. You belong to God's family. You believers are like a building that God owns. That building was built on the foundation of the apostles and prophets. Christ Jesus himself is the most important stone in that building."]* Did you catch that? The Bible says that Jesus Christ should be the cornerstone of our lives. That means that Jesus should be the most important thing in our lives. If he is, we will have a strong foundation. And if our foundation is strong, we know that when the floods and winds—the bad things that sometimes happen in everyone's life— come along, we will be strong enough to stand against them. I hope you will make Jesus the cornerstone of *your* life.

To take home: Give each child one or two of the building blocks, reminding them to think of Jesus, the Cornerstone, when they look at their blocks.

26. Ouchies and Broken Hearts

You will need: • A box of adhesive bandages

Scripture: *Psalm 147:3   He heals the brokenhearted. He bandages their wounds.*

Does anyone here happen to be wearing a bandage like this today? Can you tell me what happened that caused you to need that bandage? I cut my finger on a knife one time, and I wrapped a bandage like this around the cut. Right away the bandage helped the cut to stop bleeding; and by the time I took it off a few days later, my cut was almost healed. You know, God made us so that our bodies heal themselves when we get hurt. We may need a doctor to help set a broken bone, or we may need our mom or dad to help us put a bandage on our "ouchie"; but after that it's God who does the work, making our skin or bones grow back together and making the pain go away.

The Bible tells us that God doesn't only heal our physical "ouchies," or the hurts on our body; but when our feelings get hurt or when our hearts are broken, God can heal those kinds of hurts too. Just as it takes a while for our bodies to heal, it sometimes takes a while for hurt feelings to feel better or for broken hearts to mend. But God can do it; and if we ask, he will!

To take home: Give each child a bandage to remember the lesson by. Retailers now carry a variety of bright, colorful bandages. (If time permits, you might allow the children to open the bandages and put them around a finger or on an arm before going back to their seats, and then display these reminders of God's healing power to the congregation.)

27. The (Flash) Light of the World

You will need:
- A flashlight that takes two batteries
- Two batteries that you have labeled "HOLY SPIRIT" and "JESUS"
- A box with a lid

Scripture: *Matthew 5:14a* *"You are the light that gives light to the world."*

[Hand one of the children the flashlight (from which the batteries have been removed and hidden in the box). Ask him to turn the light on.] Oh, it's not working, is it? Hmm. I wonder why. Can you figure out why the light won't work? *[Allow the children to pass it around and let each one try to get it to work.]* Ah-ha! So that's the problem: the batteries are missing. I think I have just the solution to that problem right here in this box. The labels on these batteries say "Holy Spirit" and "Jesus." The Bible says that Christians like you and me are supposed to be the light of the world. But we are kind of like this flashlight. If we don't have

Jesus living in our hearts or the Holy Spirit working in us, we can't shine any light, can we? But when Jesus and the Holy Spirit live inside us *[put the batteries in the flashlight, and be sure the switch is on]* then we will be nice bright lights to the world so that everyone can see how much Jesus loves them. There! That's much better, isn't it? I have some small flashlights for you to take home as reminders that you, too, can be the light of the world. Could you please shine your lights over the congregation as you go back to your seats?

To take home: Let each child take home a small, inexpensive "squeeze" flashlight, usually sold alongside lightbulbs, nightlights, and so forth.

28. The Greatest Gift

You will need:
- A brightly wrapped gift box containing scripture cards
- Someone to present the gift to you at the beginning of the children's message

Scripture: *Romans 6:23b   But God gives us a free gift—life forever in Christ Jesus our Lord.*

[*Make your way to the front of the church and greet the children. Arrange ahead of time to have someone from the congregation hand you the brightly wrapped gift.*] Oh my! A gift! For me? Thank you. I think I'll just put it over here. [*Set gift aside. The giver should then ask you: "Aren't you going to open it?"*] Oh, no. It's much too pretty to open. I think I'll just leave it here. What do you children think? Should I open it? Well, all right, if you think I should. Thank you for the gift. [*The helper may be seated.*]

I *will* open this present, but first I want to tell you something very important. Jesus has a very special

gift waiting for each one of you. He has given all of
us the gift of his love and his salvation free for the
asking. But if we don't open the gift—use it and
enjoy it—it doesn't do us much good, does it? Jesus
is just waiting for us to accept his wonderful gift of
salvation. All we have to do is say, "Yes, Jesus. I want
your gift. I accept it from you, and I thank you for
it."

Now, let's find out what's in this pretty box!

To take home: Open the package and give each child a scripture
card from the gift box. Read one of the cards to the children and
the congregation. These cards may be purchased from a Christian
supply store, or you can make your own on business card-size
heavy paper. John 3:16 or Romans 6:23 are appropriate verses.

29. The Wheat and the Weeds

You will need:
- A handful of wheat
- A handful of either cheat grass or downy brome, weeds that look very much like wheat

Scripture: *Matthew 13:24-26, 30   [Jesus] said, "The kingdom of heaven is like a man who planted good seed in his field. That night, when everyone was asleep, his enemy came and planted weeds among the wheat. Then the enemy went away. Later, the wheat grew and heads of grain grew on the wheat plants. But at the same time the weeds also grew. 'Let the weeds and the wheat grow together until the harvest time. At harvest time I will tell the workers this: First gather the weeds and tie them together to be burned. Then gather the wheat and bring it to my barn.' "*

[*Show the children a handful of the weed that looks deceptively like a stalk of wheat.*] Can anyone tell me what this plant is? Some of you seem to think that this is wheat. And it does look very much like wheat, doesn't it? But guess what? It's not wheat. *This* is wheat. If you look closely you can tell that they are not the same. This first plant I showed you is actually a weed! By just glancing at this weed, it's easy to be fooled into thinking that it is wheat. Of course, if you tried to grind this weed to make flour, you would know very quickly that it is not wheat.

The Bible tells a story that Jesus told about the wheat and the weeds. It's sad to say, but there are some people who masquerade as Christians. By that, I mean that they just pretend to be Christians. They might talk like Christians, and they might try to act like Christians, but they don't really know Christ. If we knew the truth about the way they are inside, we would see that they are kind of like this weed.

It is important to make sure that we are truly following the Lord and doing the things he wants us to do.

To take home: Let each child take home a stalk of wheat.

30. Gone Fishin'

You will need:
- Fish shapes cut from colorful paper (six to eight inches in length) On each fish write "Follow me and I will make you fishermen for men." Attach a paper clip to each one.
- One or two fishing poles made by attaching a string with a magnet on the end to a stick or pole

Scripture: *Mark 1:16-18   When Jesus was walking by Lake Galilee, he saw Simon and Simon's brother, Andrew. They were fishermen and were throwing a net into the lake to catch fish. Jesus said to them, "Come and follow me. I will make you fishermen for men." So Simon and Andrew immediately left their nets and followed him.*

How would you like to go fishing this morning? We'll pretend the floor is a lake. I'll put the fish in the "lake," and give each of you a turn to catch one fish. *[Give the first two children the poles and go fishing until all have had a turn.]* Our scripture today tells us about two brothers, Simon and Andrew, who were fishermen. Fishing was their job, and, instead of poles, they used nets to catch their fish. One day while they were out on a lake, Jesus walked along the shore. He said to the two brothers, "Come and follow me. I will make you fishermen for men." Look at your fish and you will see these words on them. The Bible says that Simon and Andrew immediately left their nets and followed Jesus.

What do you think Jesus meant when he said, "I will make you fishermen for men"? Did he mean that there would be people out swimming in the lake and that Simon and Andrew would put their nets out and catch people in the net? No, I don't think this is what Jesus meant. What he was saying is that he could change Simon and Andrew's lives so much that they would no longer want to catch fish. Instead, they would want to spend their lives telling other people what a difference Jesus could make in their lives. Do you know that Jesus says these words to every one of us? He says, "Come and follow me and I will make you fishermen for men." Jesus wants each of us to follow him—to follow the ways of God—and if we do that, we can't help showing and telling others around us how Jesus has changed our lives.

To take home: Let each child take home the fish he or she caught.

31. And the Winner Is . . .

You will need: • Wide purple or blue ribbon cut into six-inch pieces
 • Gold stickers or seals on which you have written "Jesus"

Scripture: *Hebrews 12:2   Let us look only to Jesus. He is the one who began our faith, and he makes our faith perfect. Jesus suffered death on the cross. But he accepted the shame of the cross as if it were nothing. He did this because of the joy that God put before him. And now he is sitting at the right side of God's throne.*

How many of you have ever been in a race? When the gun goes off or the starter's hand goes down, what do you do? As you're running along, in which direction do you look? Well, if you want to win the race, you *should* be looking toward the finish line, shouldn't you? If you look behind you to see how many people you are ahead of, or look beside you to see who is gaining on you, it will slow you down.

Sometimes the runners in a race get a trophy or a

73

ribbon if they win the race. *[Show the children a ribbon you have made following the instructions in the* To take home *section.]*

Have you ever thought about the Christian life as a race? The writer of Hebrews did. And he said that in this race we should fix our eyes on Jesus. When Jesus lived on the earth, he had a hard race to run. He was mistreated by many people, and he even died on a cross for us. But he ran his race and he won. And because Jesus won, we can also be winners in the Christian life if we remember to keep our eyes on Jesus.

To take home: Make prize ribbons by cutting six-inch strips of ribbon and attaching a gold seal with the word "Jesus" written on it. "Maybe you can put this ribbon in your room or use it as a bookmark to remind you to always keep your eyes on Jesus."

32. When We All Get to Heaven

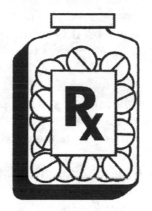

You will need: A box containing the following:
- A bottle of children's medicine, such as cough syrup
- Toothbrush
- Adhesive bandages
- Tissues
- A large portrait of Jesus

Scripture: *Revelation 21:4-5a* *"He will wipe away every tear from their eyes. There will be no more death, sadness, crying, or pain. All the old ways are gone." The One who was sitting on the throne said, "Look! I am making everything new!"*

In this box I have several things that we might need at different times. The first thing I want to show you is this bottle of medicine. When might you need this? That's right. When you are sick, sometimes you have to take medicine to help you get well. What about this toothbrush? You probably use this several times each day. It's important to brush your teeth, because if you don't, you might get cavities. How about these bandages? You might need one of these if you cut yourself or if you fall down and scrape your knee. If you are sad and there are tears streaming down your face, these tissues would come in handy to wipe your tears away. These are all important things that we use on this earth, but did you know that there will come a day when we will not need any of these things? Do you know when that will be? When we get to heaven, we will not need any of these things because Jesus has promised that in heaven there will be no more sickness, no more crying, no more sadness. In heaven, we won't even have to worry about cavities!

And Jesus is the reason that the need for all these things will come to an end. Isn't that a wonderful promise to look forward to?

To take home: Give each child a small picture of Jesus to take home. Most Christian supply stores carry wallet-sized portraits of Jesus.

33. Wear the Word

You will need: • Wear or bring jewelry with religious symbols or verses
• Plaques or posters with scripture verses

Scripture: *Deuteronomy 6:6-9   Always remember these commands I give you today. Teach them to your children. Talk about them when you sit at home and walk along the road. Talk about them when you lie down and when you get up. Write them down and tie them to your hands as a sign. Tie them on your forehead to remind you. Write them on your doors and gates.*

Long, long ago, back in Bible times, God told his people to talk about his commandments all the time. The Bible says that they were supposed to talk about the commandments when they were sitting in their houses, when they were walking along the street, when they went to bed, and when they got up. That sounds like just about all the time, doesn't it? Not only were God's people supposed to talk about the commandments, they were also supposed to decorate their houses with God's Word. We sometimes do that today, don't we? Maybe you have a picture like this hanging on the wall of your house, or maybe you have a poster something like this in your room that reminds you of Jesus. The Lord even told the people to *wear* his Word around their hands and on their foreheads. The cross on this necklace I'm wearing reminds me of Jesus. You see, God did not want his people to forget about him or to forget to keep his commandments for even a minute because God knew how important it was for people to obey the commandments that he gave them. God always knows what is best for us.

To take home: Purchase candy necklaces and double them to make bracelets. Write a scripture verse on a two-by-two-inch slip of paper. Wrap a slip around each bracelet and secure with glue. Give these to the children to wear as reminders of the things the Lord has done for them.

34. Welcome? Or Keep Out?

You will need: • Large signs that say "Welcome" and "Keep Out"

Scripture: *Psalm 122:1 I was happy when they said to me, "Let's go to the Temple of the Lord."*

Can any of you tell me what these two signs say? That's right. This long word is "welcome," and these two shorter words say "keep out." Where might you see a sign that says "keep out"? Maybe on the fence around a farmer's field, on a dangerous place like an electrical station, or on the door to your big brother or sister's bedroom. Those are all places where you might see a sign like this.

Welcome means that you would be happy to have someone come in. Where might you see a "welcome" sign? Maybe on the "welcome" mat by your neighbor's front door? Or in the front window of a store, on a sign at the city limits of your town, or maybe on a banner at a party.

Let me ask you a question. If we were to choose one of these signs to hang up in front of our church, which one do you think we should choose? I hope you would choose the welcome sign. We would like everyone to feel welcome in our church. Even if we don't have a welcome sign on our door, there are ways we can make visitors to our church feel welcome. We can stop and talk to them after church, or we can invite them to come back to our church again. Even our smiles can be like welcome signs to people who come to our church. When they see our friendly faces, they will know that we welcome them to our church, and that we hope they can feel God's love here.

To take home: Send each child home with a miniature welcome sign that can be made from poster board or construction paper.

35. Master Copy

You will need: • A picture from a book or magazine that you
have copied on a copy machine, then copied
the copy and copied that copy, and so on about
ten or twelve times

Scripture: *1 Peter 1:15-16   But be holy in all that you do, just as God
is holy. God is the One who called you. It is written in the Scriptures:
"You must be holy, because I am holy."*

Does everybody know what a copy machine is? I
took this picture from a book and used a copy
machine to make this copy. It's pretty easy to tell
which one is the copy and which one is the original.
We call the picture we started with the original. I put
this first copy back into the machine and made a
copy of the copy. Then I copied that copy and so on.
Do you see how fuzzy the picture is starting to
become? By the time I'd copied the copy about ten
times, it's hard to even tell what it's supposed to be.

The Bible tells us that we are to be holy or good, just the way that Jesus was good. Jesus is to be the one that we copy our lives after. There are a lot of good people in this world whom we could copy, and most of the time we would be doing right to follow them. But every single man or woman in the world will eventually make a mistake; and if we are looking to them as our example, we will be disappointed and maybe even led to do something that is wrong. That's why it's important that we always try to copy the original. And who is the original? That's right, it's Jesus.

To take home: Give each child a clear copy of the picture you copied to illustrate the lesson. They can take the page home and color it and hang it on their refrigerators as a reminder to copy only the original—Jesus.

3.6. Please Pass the Salt

You will need:
- A clear glass shaker of salt
- Unsalted crackers
- Crackers with salted tops
- A pitcher of cold water
- Small paper drinking cups

Scripture: *Matthew 5:13a   You are the salt of the earth.*

Do you know what I brought with me today? Usually you would see this on the table beside the pepper. That's right, it's salt. The Bible talks about salt in the book of Matthew. It says that we are the salt of the earth. We are supposed to be like salt. That sounds kind of funny, doesn't it? But when you think about some of the things that salt does, maybe it will make more sense. One of the things salt does is make things taste better. I want you to taste one of these crackers that have no salt on them, and then I'm going to give you a cracker that *has* salt, and you tell me which one you like the best. The salted one tastes better, doesn't it? You know, I think if we are "salty" like the Bible says we should be, we will make other people's lives better because they will see our kindness and our happy smiles and the good work we do, and they will know that Jesus is the one who makes us that way. Another thing about salt—it makes people thirsty! Is anyone thirsty after eating that salty cracker? Here is a drink of cold water for each of you. You see, if people see Jesus in us through our kind words and the good things we do, they will be "thirsty" to know more about God. That might give us a chance to tell them what a wonderful God we have—the God that the Bible calls *living* water! So it's not quite such a funny thing to say that we are the salt of the earth after all, is it?

To take home: Give each child a small package of salty crackers to take home or to eat quietly in church if Mom and Dad (and the janitor!) don't mind. Soup crackers work well for this.

37. Never Give Up

You will need: • Your fingers

Scripture: *Luke 18:1-8 [Tell the scripture story as your fingers act it out.]*

I want to tell you a story that Jesus told his followers. He told it to teach them that they should always pray and never give up.

Once there was a judge. *[On right hand, hold index finger up, thumb extended out, the other fingers bent down.]* He wasn't afraid of God, and he didn't care about people or about what people thought about him. In the same town there lived a woman whose husband had died. *[On left hand, hold index finger up.]* The woman came to the judge *[Walk finger to judge and wiggle it up and down as woman talks.]* and said, "There is a man who is not being fair to me. I need you to do something about it." The judge said, *[Wiggle index finger on right hand up and down as judge talks.]* "Go away and leave me alone. I don't have time to bother with you." The next day the woman came back to the judge and said, "There is a man who is not being fair to me. I need you to do something about it." But again the judge said, "Go away and leave me alone. I don't have time to bother with you." Day after day this happened. The woman would come to the judge and say, "There is a man who is not being fair to me. I need you to do something about it." And the judge would say, "Go away and leave me alone. I don't have time to bother with you."

Well, finally, after this had gone on for quite some time, the judge could take it no longer. He said, "This woman is driving me bananas! I'm not afraid of God and I don't care about people or about what people think of me, but I've got to get this woman off my back! Tomorrow when she comes, I will see that she is treated fairly."

Jesus said that if the bad judge brought fairness to the woman, won't God, who is good, give what is right to his people who pray to him day and night? Jesus said that God will help his people quickly. But we need to be sure that we are doing what God wants us to do because the story ends by asking: "When Jesus comes again will he find people on earth who believe in him?"

To take home: Cut out hand shapes by tracing around your own or a child's hand. On each one write "Always pray and never give up." You may wish to decorate them with markers, stickers, and so forth.

"Always pray and never give up."

38. Strength in Numbers

You will need:
- A large, thick phone book
- A small, thin phone book

Scripture: *Ecclesiastes* 4:12b *A rope that has three parts wrapped together is hard to break.*

I brought two books with me today. Now, usually I am very careful not to tear my books, but these phone books are old and ready to be recycled, so I don't care if they get torn. *[Choose an older child to try to tear the small book in half.]* Do you think you can rip this book in half without opening it up? Go ahead and try it. Maybe I can help you get it started. Look at that. This thin old book tore quite easily, didn't it?

Now, this big fat book is the phone book for a big city. Does anyone want to volunteer to tear this one in half? Do you think you could tear it as easily as the other one? No, I don't think so either. In fact, as hard as I try, I can't seem to make even a little tear in the book. The pages of these books are very, very thin. And one at a time they rip quite easily. But when you put many of them together, they are almost impossible to tear, aren't they?

God's people are like that. The Bible says that a rope that is made of three parts wrapped together is hard to break. This means that when we come together in the things that we believe and when we help each other and encourage each other, nothing will be able to tear us apart. One of the ways the Lord makes us strong is by giving us friends and families to help us and love us. But another important family that God gives us is our church. Just like the pieces of a rope, our church family needs to join together so we can be strong in the Lord. Let's remember how important all of God's children are to each other.

To take home: To remind the children that there is strength in numbers, braid yarn together and give each child a four-inch length of braid to use as a bookmark.

39. A Recipe for Life

You will need:
- A collection of "how-to" books, such as a set of blueprints, a cookbook, an instruction manual for an electric appliance, a baby care book, and so on.
- A Bible

Scripture: *Psalm 119:105   Your word is like a lamp for my feet and a light for my way.*

I brought some special books and papers with me today. Here is a set of blueprints that tells the carpenter how to build a house. This is a cookbook. You all know what that is for, don't you? It tells your mother or father how to make all kinds of good cakes and breads and casseroles. This is the manual that tells me how to work my washing machine. And this one is a book that tells how to take care of brand-new babies. All of these books are very important for knowing how to do a certain thing. Now, none of these "how-to" books do us any good if we just put them away on a shelf or in a drawer, do they? We must read them and follow the instructions very closely. Did you know that God has given us a very important instruction book? That book is the Bible, God's Word, and it tells us everything we need to know about the way God wants us to live our lives. But just like these other books, the Bible is meant to be read and used. If we just put it on a shelf at home and never open it up and read it, we won't know all the important things it says, will we? So let's remember to try to read this important book every day so that we can do the things God wants us to do.

To take home: Give each child a recipe card on which you have printed:

RECIPE FOR A HAPPY LIFE
A good measure of faith
A bushel of the fruits of the spirit
An overflowing cup of love
Put all ingredients in God's hands, then spread his love to everyone. Makes plenty to go around.

40. It's Nice to Share

You will need: • A bowl full of assorted candies

Scripture: *Hebrews 13:16 Do not forget to do good to others. And share with them what you have. These are the sacrifices that please God.*

[*Sit with the bowl of candy conspicuously on your lap, but do not make any reference to it. Begin to engage the children in small talk.*]

Good morning, boys and girls. Did everyone have a good week? The Lord certainly gave us a beautiful sunshiny day today, didn't he? [*Continue visiting with the children until one comments on the candy in your lap. If no one says anything, you might ask the children if anyone noticed what you have on your lap.*]

I thought you might notice that I brought this big bowl of candy with me this morning. It looks pretty tasty, doesn't it? You know, when someone has this much candy all to themselves it would really be nice if they would share, wouldn't it? I'll tell you what, I *will* share this candy with you in just a few minutes;

but first of all, I need to tell you something very important about sharing.

Did you ever think about the fact that when we have Jesus living in our hearts, we have something to share with other people that is much, much more special and important than candy? As Christians, we get to come to the church every Sunday and hear all about the wonderful things God has done for us and the wonderful gift God gave to us when he sent Jesus. But did you know that some boys and girls have never, ever heard about Jesus? There are some children—and some grown-ups too—who have never had anyone share the wonderful news about Jesus with them.

I hope that by sharing this candy with you today I will help you remember how important it is to share—not just your candy and toys and those kinds of things, but also the good news about Jesus Christ. He wants to be your best friend, and he wants you to share him with your friends so that everyone might have a chance to know him and to invite him into their lives.

To take home: Let each child choose several pieces of candy from the bowl. Ask them to share at least one piece with a friend and to also share the good news about Jesus with someone who might not know him yet.

41. Plug into the Source

You will need:
- A small table lamp
- An extension cord or an outlet at the front of the church

Scripture: *Matthew 5:16* *"You should be a light for other people. Live so that they will see the good things you do. Live so that they will praise your Father in heaven."*

I brought a lamp with me today so that we could see a little more clearly to read from the Bible this morning. I seem to be having trouble getting the lamp to turn on, though. Let's see here—I wonder what the problem could be. Oh, now I see what the problem is: the lamp isn't plugged in. You see, this is an electric lamp, and if it is not plugged into the source of power—the electric outlet—it will not work at all. *[Plug the lamp into the outlet and turn it on.]*

The Bible says that we are the light of the world. But we are just like this lamp. Unless we are plugged into the source of power, we cannot shine our light on anyone. And who do you suppose that source of power is? That's right. It is Jesus. You might wonder how we can get plugged into Jesus. When we read our Bibles, when we pray, and when we come to church to learn more about God, all of these things help us to plug into God's power.

To take home: Cut heavy paper into lightbulb shapes and print the scripture on each one. Give these to the children to remind them to plug into God's power.

42. A Clean Slate

You will need:
- A chalkboard
- A bucket of sidewalk chalk
- A chalk eraser or a damp sponge

Scripture: *Hebrews 8:12   "I will forgive them for the wicked things they did. I will not remember their sins anymore."*

Our Bible verse today talks about the way that Jesus forgives our sins. The Bible also tells us that every one of us is a sinner who needs Jesus' forgiveness. There is not one of us here in this sanctuary this morning who is perfect or who has never sinned. That's just part of being human: we make mistakes and we need to be forgiven. The wonderful news is that Jesus has made a way for our sins to not only be forgiven, but to be forgotten as well.

Let's say that this chalkboard is like our life. Almost every day we do something that we shouldn't do. Maybe we tell a lie. *[Write the word "lie"—and each other word, as you talk about it—on the board with a piece of the chalk.]* Maybe we are angry with a brother or sister or friend. Maybe we sass our mom or our dad. Maybe we cheat when we are playing a game or doing our school work. Maybe we just have a crabby attitude and we are making everyone around us miserable. All of these things are wrong and Jesus calls them sins. They mess up our life just like this chalk has messed up the nice clean chalkboard. But we don't have to go around with a messy life, piling up more and more sins and getting dirtier and dirtier with sins.

No! The good news is that Jesus wants us to tell him about the wrong things we do; and he has promised that if we just ask him, he will forgive our sins and give us a chance to be free from that old sin that makes us feel so bad. *[Erase the board completely. A large damp rag will make the board shine!]* Jesus is the only way we can truly have a clean slate.

To take home: Give each child a piece of sidewalk chalk to take home. You might say something like: "One of the nice things about sidewalk chalk is that all it takes to erase it from the sidewalk is a nice rain or a spray from the garden hose. And that might be another reminder for you of the wonderful way that Jesus washes our sins away and makes our lives clean and pure again."

43. Do You See What I Sawed?

You will need: • A saw and a piece of wood

Scripture: *Hebrews 4:12   God's word is alive and working. It is sharper than a sword sharpened on both sides. It cuts all the way into us, where the soul and the spirit are joined. It cuts to the center of our joints and our bones. And God's word judges the thoughts and feelings in our hearts.*

Can anyone tell me what job a carpenter does? That's right. A carpenter builds things. It might be a piece of furniture or even a whole house. One of the most important tools a carpenter uses is a saw. A saw is very, very sharp, so I want everyone to stand back and away from the blade while I saw this board in half. *[Saw the wood in two and show the children the cut edges.]* Do you notice how the inside of the board is ragged and broken where the saw sliced it in two? There is a scripture that talks about God's Word—the Bible—being sharper than a two-edged sword. Now, of course this isn't a sword, but it is sharp like a sword, and I think it may help us to understand just what this scripture means.

That same verse goes on to say that God's Word is able to judge the thoughts and attitudes of our heart. What this means is that sometimes when we read the Bible it helps us realize that some of the ways we think and act are not what God would want them to be. For example, suppose you have been making fun of people, saying bad things about them. Later, you might open your Bible and read these words from Ephesians: "When you talk, do not say harmful things. But say what people need—words that will help others become stronger. Then what you say will help those who listen to you." They go on to say: "Be kind and loving to each other" (4:29, 32). Do you see how God's Word can help us realize that what we did was wrong?

If we love God, we won't want to make him sad. But when the Bible shows us that we *have* done something wrong, we can be glad that God will forgive us and help us to do the right thing the next time.

Now, even though I sawed this wood in two, it can be glued or nailed back together, and it might become even stronger than it was before. God can help us to grow stronger and better if we pay attention to the "saw" of God's word.

To take home: Give each child a block of wood. You may wish to print the scripture verse on the block.

44. You're Invited

You will need: A basket filled with the following items:
- A small tablecloth
- A teapot filled with water
- Paper plates and cups
- Animal crackers
- Small party favors

Scripture: *Luke 14:12-14   Then Jesus said to the man who had invited him, "When you give a lunch or a dinner, don't invite only your friends, brothers, relatives, and rich neighbors. At another time they will invite you to eat with them. Then you will have your reward. Instead, when you give a feast, invite the poor, the crippled, the lame, and the blind. Then you will be blessed, because they cannot pay you back. They have nothing. But you will be rewarded when the good people rise from death."*

[Several days prior to this Sunday, send out invitations to a diverse group of people in your church. You might include a teenager, an elderly person, a housewife, a person of a minority group, and so on. Explain on the invita-

tion what will be happening at the children's sermon.] We have something very special planned this morning. We are going to have a tea party. I have invited some honored guests, and I would like them to join us now. While they are coming up, I am going to get the table ready. While you are eating, I would like to read a story Jesus told. *[Read scripture.]*

When you boys and girls want to have someone over to play, whom are you most likely to invite? Most often we like to invite the people we have the most fun with. And many times these are people who are our own age and people who will probably invite us over to their houses sometime. Children, teenagers, and adults of all ages all seem to do this. But if we do what Jesus said to do, we will try to reach out to people who might have less to be thankful for than we do. Jesus said to invite the poor, the crippled, and the blind. Maybe for you that will mean playing with that shy boy or girl at recess instead of your favorite friends. Maybe it will mean inviting someone to your party whom no one else has invited to their party. The people I invited to our party this morning are probably very different from you, but we are all happy they could be at our party. I hope that you will make an effort this week to be a friend to a person who needs a friend.

To take home: Let each child take home a party favor from the tea table.

45. There's No Place Like Home

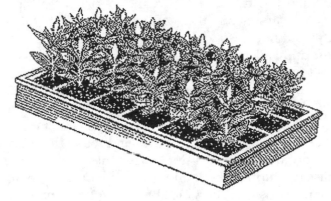

You will need:
- An elementary science book or encyclopedia showing the stages of a seed's growth
- A bean or other seed

Scripture: *Philippians 3:20-21a   But our homeland is in heaven, and we are waiting for our Savior, the Lord Jesus Christ, to come from heaven. He will change our simple bodies and make them like his own glorious body.*

[Show children the seed.] Who can tell me what this is? What would happen to this seed if we planted it in the ground at the right time of year and it got plenty of water and sunshine? That's right. It would grow into a plant, wouldn't it?

I brought a book that shows the stages of a seed's growth. First the seed is planted. After it lies in the ground for a while, its coat or outside splits open and a tiny plant inside the seed breaks through the seed coat. As it grows, a root reaches down into the soil and the plant pushes up through the ground.

Now keep this picture in mind while I read our Bible verses. *[Read scripture.]* I would like for you to think of this little seed in the ground as your life here on earth. We have many good things here on earth, don't we? We have families that love us, good food to eat, and warm houses to live in. This seed looks pretty cozy snuggled in the warm soil, doesn't it? Maybe it would like to stay tucked in the ground where it is safe and warm. But that is not what the seed was created for. The seed was created to grow into a plant. And did you know that people weren't created to stay on earth forever? The Bible says that our homeland is in heaven, and that when Jesus Christ comes back he will change our bodies and make them like his glorious body. Just think what the seed would miss if it didn't sprout and grow. It wouldn't get to see the sunshine and blue sky or feel the gentle breeze or grow into a beautiful green plant. And just think what we would miss out on if we stayed on earth forever. We would miss the beautiful homeland Jesus is making ready for us in heaven.

To take home: Plant bean seeds in paper cups for the children to take home and watch grow into plants. As an alternative, you could give each child a packet of (non-poisonous) flower seeds to plant at home.

46. This Is My Commandment

You will need: • The word "commandment" printed on a piece of heavy paper. On the back of the paper make as many other words as you can from the word "commandment."
• A piece of paper and a pencil

Scripture: *Matthew 22:35-40   One Pharisee was an expert in the law of Moses. That Pharisee asked Jesus a question to test him. The Pharisee asked, "Teacher, which command in the law is the most important?" Jesus answered, " 'Love the Lord your God with all your heart, soul, and mind.' This is the first and most important command. And the second command is like the first: 'Love your neighbor as you love yourself.' All the law and the writings of the prophets depend on these two commands."*

Who can tell me what this big word is? That's right: commandment. A commandment is a rule or order that God has given us. Let's play a game using this word. Let's see how many words we can make using the letters from the big word *commandment*.

[Help the children find several smaller words within the larger one.] If we had more time, we could probably find even more words. When I did this at home, I came up with more than forty different words just using these letters.

In the scripture reading today, a man who knew a lot about the laws of God asked Jesus a trick question. Listen to how Jesus answered that question. *[Read scripture.]*

In the Bible there are many commandments that God has given. It would be almost impossible to memorize all of these. But I'll bet we can all remember "Love God and love your neighbor." Can you say that with me? Did you know that if we obeyed just these two commandments, we would never break any of God's other laws? If we always loved God with all our heart, soul, and mind, and if we always loved our neighbor as much as we love ourselves, we would automatically be keeping all the other laws God gave us.

It's a little like these words we made. All of the letters are found in the one word. It would be hard to memorize this whole list of words, but we can easily remember the one word *commandment*. In the same way, if we can keep Jesus' words—"love God and love your neighbor"—always in our hearts and minds, we will do well.

To take home: Give each child a purchased or homemade word puzzle with a biblical theme.

47. What's in a Name?*

NAMES

You will need: • A book that lists names and their meanings

Scripture: *Matthew 1:23b "And they will name him Immanuel."
This name means "God is with us."*

Each one of you boys and girls has a name, don't
you? Your name is something that sets you apart
from every other boy and girl. I am sure that long
before you were born your parents started thinking
about the name they wanted to give you. They probably chose one name in case you were a girl and
another in case you turned out to be a boy. You can
be sure that they gave a lot of thought to what they
would name you. Some of you might be named after
a grandfather or a grandmother or some other rela-
tive. But I'm sure that whatever name your parents
chose for you, they thought it was the most beautiful
name in the whole world. Did you know that names
have meanings? I brought a book with me that tells

*This sermon could also be used for Advent.

the meanings of some names. Let's look up some of your names and see what they mean.

The Bible tells us that God gave Jesus a very special name also. God gave his son the name Immanuel, which means "God with us." That is very important because God sent Jesus to earth as a human. But even though Jesus was a man, he was also God, and his name tells us that. Our names are very important to God too. And there is a wonderful secret about our names that the Bible tells us in Revelation. This is the secret: God has a book called the Book of Life; and if you love Jesus and live your life for him, your name is written down in that wonderful book.

To take home: If you know the children's names ahead of time, make up little cards telling the meaning of each name for them to take home. Be sure to have something special for visitors or new children to take home as well (possibly blank cards on which you can write their names).

48. Super Bowl Sunday

You will need: • A football and a football helmet

Scripture: *Ephesians 6:10, 12-13, 17a   Finally, be strong in the Lord and in his great power. Our fight is not against people on earth.... We are fighting against the spiritual powers of evil in the heavenly world. That is why you need to get God's full armor. Then on the day of evil you will be able to stand strong. And when you have finished the whole fight, you will still be standing. Accept God's salvation to be your helmet.*

Today is a special Sunday for anyone who loves football. It's Super Bowl Sunday, isn't it? This is a day when the two very best football teams in the whole United States come together and play a game to see who is the champion of all. *[At this point you might name the teams who are playing this year.]* The game will be on television so everyone will have a chance to watch it, even if they can't actually be in the stadium.

Now as you can imagine, both of these teams really

want to win this game. They have been practicing for weeks and weeks. Since football is a rough sport, all of the players wear special uniforms with thick pads and helmets to protect their bodies and heads.

Did you know that we are on a team too? It's not a football team. On our team Jesus is the coach and we as Christians are the players. The goal of our team is to do everything we can to help other people decide to be on Jesus' team. How can we be on Jesus' team? If you love Jesus and have asked him to come into your heart, the Bible says that God gives us a special helmet—the helmet of salvation.

Now, we have no way of knowing who will win the Super Bowl today. But did you know that the Bible already tells us that Jesus is going to win the game? The Bible promises us that Christians will win the very important game (or battle) between good and evil. I don't know about you, but I want to be on that team—the winning team.

To take home: Party goods stores carry miniature plastic football helmets. These can serve as reminders that we want to be on God's team.

49. He's Alive!

You will need:
- A piece of paper
- A living plant or potted flower

Scripture: *Romans 6:10-11   Yes, when Christ died, he died to defeat the power of sin one time—enough for all time. He now has a new life, and his new life is with God. In the same way, you should see yourselves as being dead to the power of sin and alive with God through Christ Jesus.*

I brought two objects with me this morning. I have a piece of paper and a plant. Who can tell me which object is alive? That's right. The plant is alive. But the paper came from something that was once alive. Who can tell me what that might be? Right, a tree. Tell me why a tree is alive and paper is not. (A tree grows; paper does not. A tree can make another little tree when a seed drops into the ground; this piece of paper cannot make another little piece of paper, can it? A tree can lose its leaves and new ones will grow back; this paper will always stay like this.) Would you rather be something that isn't living, like a piece of paper, or something that is alive, like a tree?

Today is Easter Sunday. Because of what Jesus did for us on the cross, we have a choice of remaining dead in our sins or being alive with Christ. Listen to what the Bible says. *[Read scripture.]* If you accept the wonderful gift of love that God has given in his son Jesus Christ, this is a wonderful day to be alive!

To take home: Buy flats of small potted flowers. Cut the sections apart and give each child a potted flower.

50. Father's Day*

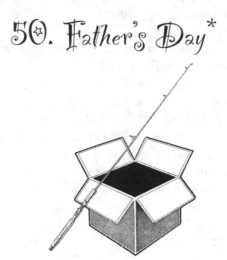

You will need:
- Large cardboard box (like a refrigerator box or large packing box)
- A small gift for each father in the congregation (suggested items: bags of peanuts or candy, packs of gum or mints, combs, key chains, notepads, etc.)
- Homemade fishing pole(s) with a clothespin hook
- A teenager or other helper to bait the hook from inside the box

Scripture: *Exodus 20:12a   Honor your father and your mother.*

What special day is it today? What are some things that your fathers like to do in their spare time? Do you ever get to do these things with your dads? It's pretty neat when you get to go on an outing or do something special with Dad, isn't it? I grew up on a

*Moms like to fish too! This sermon could easily be adapted for Mother's Day!

farm and used to get to ride on the tractor with my dad and help feed cattle or bale hay. *[Share your own stories of time spent with your father.]* I still enjoy doing things with my dad.

God had a wonderful plan when he gave us fathers. The Bible tells us to honor—or respect—our fathers and mothers. It also says to obey them. I think it would also be a good idea for each of you to pray for your fathers. Most fathers try to do the best job they can in raising you. But all parents need God's help to do the job.

We're going to do something now that lots of dads like to do. We're going to go fishing and see if we can catch a little something for you to give your dad. Then we'll pass out some treats to the other men in the congregation.

To take home: Each child will give their own father the gift they "caught." Ask two or three of the children to pass out gifts to the other men in the congregation. You might say: "Would all the men of the church please stand? Perhaps you're not a father but you've made a difference in someone else's life. We would like to honor you today, as well."

51. The Red, White, and Blue

You will need:
- A cake decorated for Independence Day
- A fork

Scripture: *Galatians 5:13   My brothers, God called you to be free. But do not use your freedom as an excuse to do the things that please your sinful self. Serve each other with love.*

Who can tell me what holiday we will be celebrating this week? That's right. It will soon be the fourth of July, which is Independence Day. That is the day our country, America, gained its independence from England. We became a free country. Our Bible verse this morning talks about freedom. *[Read verse.]*

I brought a special Independence Day cake with me this morning. How many of you like cake? *[Hand a fork to one of the children.]* What if I told you that you could take this fork and eat this whole cake right here and now? That's not something you usually get to do, is it? Well, I'm not going to let you do it this morning either! But if I had given you permission, we could say that you had the freedom to eat the cake. Do you think eating the whole cake would be the best thing for you to do? Why not? That's right. You might get sick! And if you ate the whole cake by yourself, there wouldn't be any left for the rest of us, would there? The Bible tells us that we should never use our freedom just to make ourselves happy. Instead, we should serve each other with love and think of other people. Freedom is a wonderful gift when we use it the way God intended it to be used.

To take home: Purchase individually wrapped snack cakes and place a flag sticker on top of each one. Ask the children not to open the cakes until they get home (or you might hand them out after church instead).

52. The Reason for the Season

You will need: • A sanctuary newly decorated for Christmas

Scripture: *Revelation 22:20b:* *[Jesus] says, "Yes, I am coming soon."* *Amen.*

Do you notice anything different about our church this morning? This is the beginning of what we call the Advent season. *Advent* is a word that means "arrival," and for Christians it is a time of excitement and anxious waiting as we get ready for Christmas to arrive. As you look around the sanctuary this morning, what are some of the decorations you see that tell you Christmas is coming? (Purple paraments, decorated tree, poinsettias, lights, etc.) We will be doing some special things in our church during the Advent season. We will light candles in the Advent wreath and sing special Christmas carols that we only sing during this time of year.

Some of you are probably getting excited about Christmas. Presents, parties, and putting up special decorations are all ways that we celebrate the holiday. But we should be careful not to get so excited about all those things that we forget the real reason we celebrate Christmas. We need to be excited because Jesus is coming!

We all know that a long, long time ago, Jesus came to earth as a baby and grew up to be a man. He died on the cross and rose from the dead so that if we believe in him, we could all be with him in heaven someday. So what am I talking about when I say that we need to be excited about Jesus coming? I'm talking about Jesus coming to live in our hearts and in our lives. We could crowd him out this Christmas if we only think about all the presents we want or the candy we'll get. But Jesus wants us to make room for him. One way we can make room for Christ is by remembering the real reason for Christmas every time we see a decoration or hear a Christmas carol. As Christmas comes closer and closer, I hope you will remind yourself each day that Jesus is coming. Be sure that there is room in your heart for him!

To take home: Give the children a simple Christmas ornament with a religious theme to remind them of the real reason for the season.

INDEX OF SCRIPTURES

TOPICAL INDEX